Early
ANIMAL
Encyclopedias

DOGS

by Marie-Therese Miller, PhD

Early Encyclopedias

An Imprint of Abdo Reference
abdobooks.com

abdobooks.com

Published by Abdo Reference, a division of ABDO, PO Box 398166, Minneapolis, Minnesota 55439.
Copyright © 2023 by Abdo Consulting Group, Inc. International copyrights reserved in all countries.
No part of this book may be reproduced in any form without written permission from the
publisher. Early Encyclopedias™ is a trademark and logo of Abdo Reference.

Printed in the United States of America, North Mankato, Minnesota.
102022
012023

Editor: Marie Pearson
Series Designers: Candice Keimig, Joshua Olson

Library of Congress Control Number: 2022940674

Publisher's Cataloging-in-Publication Data

Names: Miller, Marie-Therese, author.
Title: Dogs / by Marie-Therese Miller
Description: Minneapolis, Minnesota: Abdo Publishing, 2023 | Series: Early animal encyclopedias |
        Includes online resources and index.
Identifiers: ISBN 9781098290412 (lib. bdg.) | ISBN 9781098275730 (ebook)
Subjects: LCSH: Dogs--Juvenile literature. | Dogs--Behavior--Juvenile literature. | Zoology--Juvenile
        literature. | Encyclopedias and dictionaries--Juvenile literature.
Classification: DDC 636.7--dc23

CONTENTS

Dog breeds come in many shapes and sizes.

Dog Breed Groups

The American Kennel Club (AKC) keeps records of dogs. It also offers dog shows and dog sports. The AKC puts dogs into seven main groups. These are the Herding, Hound, Non-Sporting, Sporting, Terrier, Toy, and Working Groups.

Herding dogs keep groups of animals together. They move the groups from one place to another. Hounds are hunting dogs. Some hounds use their sensitive noses to find prey. Other hounds chase prey at high speeds.

The Non-Sporting Group has dogs that do not fit well in the other groups. Some have jobs that no other breed has. Dogs in the Sporting Group help hunters. The dog will find prey and bring it back to the hunter. Terriers hunt small prey. They dig to hunt animals such as rats or badgers. Dogs in the Toy Group are small. They are loving. Working Group dogs do jobs that help people. Some pull sleds. Others rescue people in the water.

The blend of white and colored furs is called ticking.

Australian Cattle Dog

AKC Date: 1980

Appearance

The Australian cattle dog is muscular. It has a smooth double coat. The coat can be black or red with white hairs mixed in. The black-and-white

Height: 🜚
17 to 20 inches
(43 to 51 cm) at the
shoulders

Weight: ⚖
35 to 50 pounds
(16 to 23 kg)

blend looks blue. That is why the dogs are often called blue heelers. They have bushy tails. Their ears are pricked.

Behavior

These dogs were bred to herd cattle. They are smart and brave. They like to stay busy. Herding trials and dog sports are good ways to keep them active.

Coral Sea

Australia

Indian
Ocean

Pacific
Ocean

From: Australia

Australian shepherds often have tan and white markings.

Australian Shepherd

AKC Date: 1991

Appearance

The Australian shepherd (Aussie) has a medium-length double coat. The coat can be black or red. Or it can be red or blue merle. Some Australian shepherds have blue eyes.

These dogs can be born with short tails. Others have their tails docked.

Behavior

These dogs are smart and full of energy. They are easy to train. They want to keep busy with a job. Working Aussies herd sheep, cattle, and other livestock. Pet Aussies sometimes herd family pets and children!

Height:
18 to 23 inches
(46 to 58 cm) at the shoulders

Weight:
40 to 65 pounds
(18 to 29 kg)

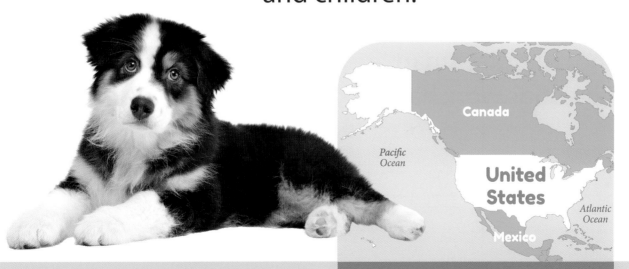

From: The United States of America

Bergamasco Sheepdog

AKC Date: 2015

Appearance

Bergamasco sheepdogs are large and muscular. They have long, wooly, corded coats. The coats can be gray or black.

Behavior

Bergamasco sheepdogs herd and guard sheep. They protect their families too. They are smart. The dogs work hard.

Height:
22 to 23.5 inches (56 to 60 cm) at the shoulders

Weight:
57 to 84 pounds (26 to 38 kg)

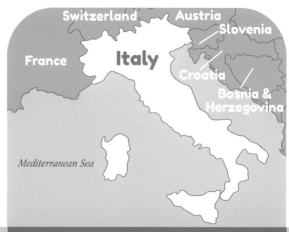

From: Italy

Border Collie

AKC Date: 1995

Appearance

Border collies have double coats. The coats can be long or short. Often, Border collies are black and white. They come in many other colors and patterns too.

Height:
18 to 22 inches (46 to 56 cm) at the shoulders

Weight:
30 to 55 pounds (14 to 25 kg)

Behavior

Border collies are very smart. They can learn many commands. These dogs are good at herding sheep. They have lots of energy. They do well in dog sports.

Atlantic Ocean
Scotland
Northern Ireland
Ireland
England
Wales

From: England and Scotland

Collies became famous when the breed starred as Lassie in films during the mid-1900s.

Collie

AKC Date: 1885

Appearance

Collies have long, narrow heads. Their ears are half pricked and fold over at the tips. Some collies have long fur. This is called a rough coat.

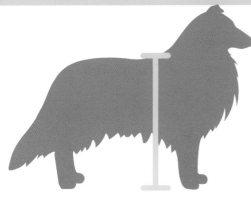

Height: 🈂
22 to 26 inches
(56 to 66 cm) at the
shoulders

Weight: ⚖
50 to 75 pounds
(23 to 34 kg)

Other collies have short fur. This is called a smooth coat. Both types of coats come in sable and white; black, white, and tan; or blue merle. Collies can also be mostly white.

Behavior

Collies are friendly and loyal. They are smart and enjoy training. Collies are gentle with children. They bark a lot. They make good watchdogs.

From: England and Scotland

German Shepherd Dog

AKC Date: 1908

Appearance

German shepherd dogs are large and muscular. They have medium-length

German shepherds need a lot of exercise.

From: Germany

Height:
22 to 26 inches
(56 to 66 cm) at the
shoulders

Weight:
50 to 90 pounds
(23 to 41 kg)

double coats. Many are black and tan. But they can be other colors too, from white to black. Their ears are pricked. They have bushy tails.

Behavior

German shepherds were bred to herd sheep. They are very smart. They are fast and powerful. Many are brave and protective. They often work with the police and military. These dogs sometimes work as guide dogs for people who are blind.

Pembrokes' ears are round at the tips.

Pembroke Welsh Corgi

AKC Date: 1934

Appearance

Pembroke Welsh corgis have long bodies and short legs. The Pembroke has a medium-length double coat. It sheds a lot. Coat colors are black

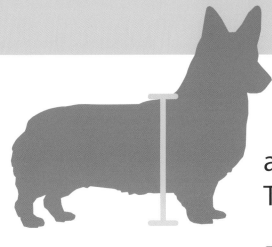

Height:
10 to 12 inches
(25 to 31 cm) at the shoulders

Weight:
up to 30 pounds
(14 kg)

and tan, fawn, red, and sable. These dogs' ears prick up.

Behavior

Pembroke Welsh corgis were bred to herd cattle. Without training, they may try to herd people. They are smart and easy to train. Pembrokes need to stay active. They are friendly and loyal. They are brave. These dogs bark a lot.

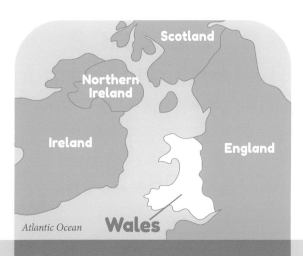

From: Wales

Shetland sheepdogs are small, but they need a lot of exercise.

Shetland Sheepdog

AKC Date: 1911

Appearance

The Shetland sheepdog (Sheltie) has a long, thick double coat. The coat comes in black, sable, and blue merle. These dogs can have white and tan markings. Shelties have long, thin faces.

Height: 13 to 16 inches (33 to 41 cm) at the shoulders

Weight: 15 to 25 pounds (7 to 11 kg)

Their ears are half pricked and fold over at the tips.

Behavior

Shetland sheepdogs were bred to herd sheep and farm birds. They are smart and obedient. They are agile. They do well in dog sports. Shelties bark a lot. Like other herding breeds, they may chase things that move quickly, like cars.

Scotland

Northern Ireland

Ireland

England

Wales

Atlantic Ocean

From: Scotland

Bouvier des Flandres

From: Belgium and France

Behavior: Bouvier des Flandres (BOO-vee-ay DUH FLAN-duhrs) can herd cattle and pull carts. They are brave guard dogs.

Briard

From: France

Behavior: Briards are herding and guardian dogs. They are smart.

Finnish Lapphund

From: Finland

Behavior: Finnish Lapphunds were bred to herd reindeer. They are very friendly and loyal. They bark a lot.

Miniature American Shepherd

From: The United States of America

Behavior: Miniature American shepherds want to work. They are very smart and energetic.

Old English Sheepdog

From: England

Behavior: Old English sheepdogs like to play. They are good with kids. They are smart. Sheepdogs are loud barkers.

Puli

From: Hungary

Behavior: A puli (PU-lee) will herd children and pets. These dogs are smart. They are very agile. They make good watchdogs.

Some Afghan hounds have beards, and some do not.

Afghan Hound

AKC Date: 1926

Appearance

The Afghan hound has short fur on its face and back. The rest of the body has long, silky fur. The coat

Uzbekistan

Turkmenistan

Tajikistan

Iran

Afghanistan

Pakistan

From: Afghanistan and surrounding area

Height: 25 to 27 inches
(64 to 69 cm) at the
shoulders

Weight: 50 to 60 pounds
(23 to 27 kg)

comes in many colors.
These dogs have long,
thin heads. Their floppy
ears are long. Their feet
are large.

Behavior

Afghan hounds are sight
hounds. They have a
strong prey drive. This
means they will chase
animals. Afghans are
independent. They move
quickly. They are agile.
Many like lure coursing. In
this sport, the dog chases
a plastic bag pulled along
the ground.

A beagle may not listen to its owner if it catches a scent.

Beagle

AKC Date: 1885

Appearance

Beagles have long, floppy ears. They have short, smooth coats. The coats can

Scotland

Northern Ireland

Ireland

England

Wales

Atlantic Ocean

From: England

have two colors or three colors together. Beagles come in two different sizes.

Behavior

Beagles are scent hounds. They often hunt rabbits. They will chase small animals. Beagles have lots of energy. They are friendly and happy. They love their families. They do well with other dogs. They are loud barkers.

Height:
Under 13 inches (33 cm) at the shoulders
13 to 15 inches (33 to 38 cm) at the shoulders

Weight:
Under 20 pounds (9 kg)
20 to 30 pounds (9 to 14 kg)

Bloodhound

AKC Date: 1885

The bloodhound's powerful legs allow it to walk for miles following scents.

Appearance

Bloodhounds are muscular. They have long ears that hang down. They have loose skin with many folds on the face. Bloodhounds have short coats. The coats can be black and tan, liver and tan, or red.

Height: 🖹
23 to 27 inches
(58 to 69 cm) at the
shoulders

Weight: ⚖
80 to
110 pounds
(36 to 50 kg)

Behavior
Bloodhounds have an amazing sense of smell. They can find lost people using their noses. They often work as search and rescue dogs and as police dogs. Bloodhounds are smart. They are friendly and gentle. They drool a lot.

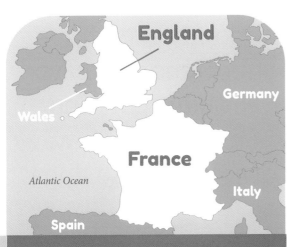

From: England and France

Dachshund

AKC Date: 1885

Dachshunds often bond closely with one person.

Appearance

Dachshunds have short legs and long bodies. They have long, floppy ears. Smooth dachshunds have short, smooth coats. Wirehaired dachshunds have rough coats and beards. Longhaired dachshunds have long, wavy fur. The coats come in lots of colors. These dogs

come in miniature or standard size.

Height:
Miniature: 5 to 6 inches (13 to 15 cm) at the shoulders
Standard: 8 to 9 inches (20 to 23 cm) at the shoulders

Weight:
Miniature: 11 pounds (5 kg)
Standard: 16 to 32 pounds (7 to 15 kg)

Behavior

Dachshunds were bred to hunt badgers. They also hunt rabbits. They are brave and smart. They like to dig and bark.

From: Germany

Greyhound

AKC Date: 1885

Appearance

Greyhounds have long, narrow bodies. Their fur is short and smooth. It comes in many different colors.

Behavior

Greyhounds are sight hounds. They are very fast and agile. They can run 45 miles per hour (72 kmh). These dogs will chase small animals. Greyhounds are gentle. They are good with families.

Height:
27 to 30 inches (69 to 76 cm) at the shoulders

Weight:
60 to 70 pounds (27 to 32 kg)

Mediterranean Sea

Israel

Libya

Egypt

Saudi Arabia

Sudan

From: Egypt and the surrounding area

Irish Wolfhound

AKC Date: 1897

Appearance

Irish wolfhounds are the tallest of the AKC breeds. The wolfhound has a rough, wiry double coat. The coat comes in many colors, including gray and fawn.

Height:
30 to 32 inches (76 to 81 cm) at the shoulders

Weight:
105 to 120 pounds (48 to 54 kg)

Behavior

Irish wolfhounds are sight hounds. They hunted large animals such as wolves. Irish wolfhounds are calm. They are usually quiet.

Northern Ireland

Ireland

Great Britain

Atlantic Ocean

From: Ireland and Northern Ireland

Rhodesian ridgebacks need a fenced area to run in.

Rhodesian Ridgeback

AKC Date: 1955

Appearance

The Rhodesian ridgeback can have a ridge of fur down its back. The fur grows toward the head instead of toward the tail. The dog's coat is short and smooth. It comes in shades of wheat from golden to red. These dogs are muscular.

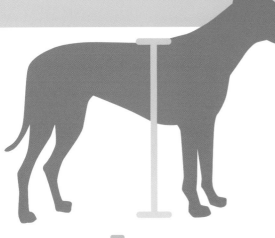

Height:
24 to 27 inches
(61 to 69 cm) at the
shoulders

Weight:
70 to 85 pounds
(32 to 39 kg)

Behavior

Rhodesian ridgebacks were bred to hunt large animals in Africa. They were even used in lion hunts. They will chase animals. Rhodesian ridgebacks love their families. They are protectors. Ridgebacks take a while to make friends with new people. They are calm indoors.

From: Zimbabwe

Whippets enjoy lying on couches, beds, and other comfy places.

Whippet

AKC Date: 1888

Appearance

The whippet has a long, thin head. It also has a long neck and thin legs. The tail is long too. This breed's coat is short and smooth. It comes in many colors and patterns, including brindle. Its back legs are powerful.

Height: 18 to 22 inches
(46 to 56 cm) at the shoulders

Weight: 25 to 40 pounds
(11 to 18 kg)

Behavior

Whippets are sight hounds. They will chase small animals. They are very fast runners and do well in dog sports. Many play with balls or disks. Whippets are friendly and gentle. They are calm and quiet indoors. They are good with gentle kids.

Scotland

Northern
Ireland

Ireland

England

Wales

Atlantic Ocean

From: England

Basenji

From: Central Africa

Behavior: Basenjis are fast. They are smart and independent. These dogs do not bark, but they make other noises.

Basset Hound

From: Belgium and France

Behavior: Basset hounds are scent hounds. They are gentle. They are friendly and loyal.

Norwegian Elkhound

From: Norway

Behavior: Norwegian elkhounds hunt moose. They are brave and loyal. They make good watchdogs.

Portuguese Podengo Pequeno

From: Portugal

Behavior: These small dogs are playful. They are loving with their families. They make good watchdogs.

Saluki

From: The Middle East

Behavior: Salukis are fast and agile. They are independent.

Scottish Deerhound

From: Scotland

Behavior: These tall sight hounds were used to hunt deer. They are brave. These dogs are gentle and loving.

Bichons need frequent haircuts.

Bichon Frise

AKC Date: 1972

Appearance

The bichon frise (bee-SHAWN free-ZAY) has a curly coat. The dog looks like a powder puff. The coat is white. It can have shades of apricot, buff, or cream. This dog's nose is black, and the eyes are dark. The tail curls over the back.

Height:
9.5 to
11.5 inches
(24.1 to 29.2 cm) at
the shoulders

Weight:
12 to 18 pounds
(5 to 8 kg)

Behavior

The bichon frise is a playful dog. These dogs are smart and easy to train. They love to perform. They are friendly and can be good with kids and dogs. Bichons are good watchdogs.

From: Belgium and France

The Boston terrier's nickname is the "American gentleman."

Boston Terrier

AKC Date: 1893

Appearance

Boston terriers are muscular. They have short muzzles and short tails. The coat is smooth

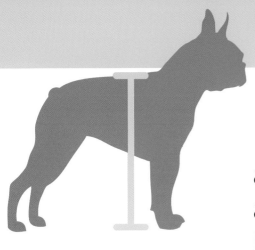

Height:
15 to 17 inches (38 to 43 cm) at the shoulders

Weight:
12 to 25 pounds (5 to 11 kg)

and short. The fur looks like a tuxedo coat. It comes in brindle, black, and dark brown with white markings. These dogs' eyes are large and round. They have pricked ears.

Behavior

Boston terriers are smart. They are friendly. These dogs do not do well being alone a lot. They are loving with their families. They are good with kids.

From: The United States of America

A bulldog's wrinkles need to be cleaned often.

Bulldog

AKC Date: 1886

Appearance

Bulldogs are stocky. This breed has a short muzzle and wrinkles on the face and head. The bulldog has an underbite. The coat is short and smooth. It comes in red, white, and fawn. The coat can have many patterns.

Height: 14 to 15 inches (36 to 38 cm) at the shoulders

Weight: 40 to 50 pounds (18 to 23 kg)

Bulldogs have small ears and short tails.

Behavior

Bulldogs are brave and friendly. They are loving with their families. The bulldog is calm, but it still needs exercise. The breed can easily overheat in hot weather. Exercising in cool parts of the day is best.

Scotland

Northern Ireland

Ireland

England

Wales

Atlantic Ocean

From: England

Chinese Shar-Pei

AKC Date: 1992

Appearance

The Chinese shar-pei has wrinkled skin and a wide muzzle. This dog has a blue-black tongue. It has short, sandpapery fur. The coat comes in many colors.

Behavior

Shar-peis are brave. They are calm and can live in apartments. They are loyal to their families. These dogs are smart but can be difficult to train.

Height:
18 to 20 inches (46 to 51 cm) at the shoulders

Weight:
45 to 60 pounds (20 to 27 kg)

From: China

Dalmatian

AKC Date: 1888

Appearance

Dalmatians are white with black or liver spots. The coat is short and smooth. They are muscular dogs.

Height: 19 to 24 inches (48 to 61 cm) at the shoulders

Weight: 45 to 70 pounds (20 to 32 kg)

Behavior

Dalmatians were used with horse-drawn coaches. They cleared a path for the horses and guarded them. Dalmatians need to keep busy. They are loving with their families.

From: Unknown

French
bulldogs
snore.

French Bulldog

AKC Date: 1898

Appearance

French bulldogs are stocky. They have short
muzzles. There are wrinkles around the nose. The
breed has large, bat-like ears and an underbite.
It has a short coat. The fur comes in mixes of

Height: 11 to 13 inches (28 to 33 cm) at the shoulders

Weight: Under 28 pounds (13 kg)

brindle, white, cream, and fawn. It can have many types of markings. The dog has a short tail.

Behavior

French bulldogs were bred to be companion dogs. They are playful without being very energetic. They are loving with families. These dogs are good with kids. They make fine watchdogs.

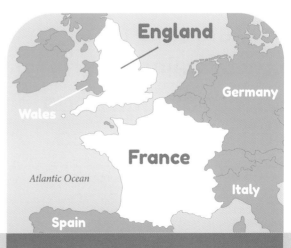

England

Germany

Wales

France

Atlantic Ocean

Italy

Spain

From: England and France

Keeshond

AKC Date: 1930

Appearance

The Keeshond (KAYS-hawnd) has dark markings on the face that look like eyeglasses. This dog has a curled tail. The coat comes in mixtures of black, silver, gray, and cream.

Height:
17 to 18 inches
(43 to 46 cm) at the shoulders

Weight:
35 to 45 pounds
(16 to 20 kg)

Behavior

These dogs were watchdogs on boats and farms. They are smart and easy to train. They are friendly and good with kids. This breed barks loudly.

The Netherlands

North Sea

Germany

Belgium

From: The Netherlands

Lhasa Apso

AKC Date: 1935

Appearance

Lhasa apsos have long fur. It parts in the middle of the back. The coat comes in many colors and patterns. The Lhasa holds its tail high above its back. The tail curls.

Behavior

Lhasa apsos were used as watchdogs. They are brave and smart. They are loyal.

Height: 10 to 11 inches (25 to 28 cm) at the shoulders

Weight: 12 to 18 pounds (5 to 8 kg)

From: Tibet, China

A poodle's fur does not shed.

Poodle (Miniature and Standard)

AKC Date: 1887

Appearance

Poodles have long, curly fur. It can be cut in many ways. The fur

From: Germany

Height: 📏

Miniature: 10 to 15 inches
(25 to 38 cm) at the shoulders

Standard: more than 15 inches
(38 cm) at the shoulders

Weight: ⚖️

Miniature: 10 to 15 pounds
(5 to 7 kg)

Standard: 40 to 70 pounds
(18 to 32 kg)

comes in many colors. These include black, white, and apricot. Poodles have long muzzles. The Non-Sporting Group has two sizes of poodle, the miniature and the standard.

Behavior

Poodles retrieve ducks. Poodles are smart and easy to train. They are active and friendly. Poodles get along with children.

Many Shiba Inus today are still great hunters.

Shiba Inu

AKC Date: 1992

Appearance

Shiba Inus (SHEE-bah EE-noos) are muscular. They have triangle-shaped ears. Their fluffy tails curl over their backs. These dogs have thick double coats. The colors are black and tan,

cream, red, and red sesame. Coats can have white or cream markings. Shibas shed a lot.

Behavior

Shiba Inus were bred to hunt. They are brave and independent. They can be difficult to train. Shibas are loyal. They do not always get along with other dogs.

Height:
13.5 to 16.5 inches
(34.3 to 41.9 cm) at the shoulders

Weight:
17 to 23 pounds
(8 to 10 kg)

Russia
North Korea
China
Sea of Japan
South Korea
Japan
Pacific Ocean

From: Japan

Chow Chow

From: China

Behavior: These dogs are smart and independent. Chow chows keep themselves clean.

Coton de Tulear

From: Madagascar

Behavior: The little Coton de Tulear (co-TAWN DAY too-LEE-are) is smart. It is easy to train.

Finnish Spitz

From: Finland

Behavior: The Finnish spitz hunts birds. It barks to tell hunters where prey is. These dogs are friendly and busy.

Schipperke

From: Belgium

Behavior: The schipperke (SKIH-per-key) hunted rats on boats. These dogs are independent and energetic.

Tibetan Terrier

From: Tibet, China

Behavior: Tibetan terriers are good watchdogs. They are loving and loyal to their families.

Xoloitzcuintli

From: Mexico

Behavior: The Xoloitzcuintli (show-low-eets-QUEENT-lee) is loyal to its owner. It will chase animals. These dogs can be hairless. They like to keep clean.

Besides pointing, the Brittany also retrieves.

Brittany

AKC Date: 1934

Appearance

Brittanys have double coats with light feathering. They are wavy and thick enough to protect the dogs from sharp plants. The coat is usually white with orange or liver markings. These dogs' tails are naturally short or docked. Their floppy ears are shaped like triangles.

Height: 🗒
17.5 to
20.5 inches
(44.5 to 52.1 cm) at
the shoulders

Weight: ⚖
30 to 40 pounds
(14 to 18 kg)

Behavior

Brittanys often help bird hunters. They freeze and point when they find birds. These dogs are easy to train. They have lots of energy and need exercise. They are friendly and love people. Brittanys do well in dog sports.

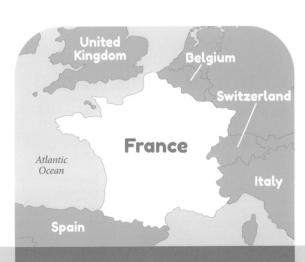

From: France

The cocker spaniel is the smallest breed in AKC's Sporting Group.

Cocker Spaniel

AKC Date: 1878

Appearance

Cocker spaniels have big eyes. Their long ears hang down. They have short docked tails. These dogs also have long double coats. Cockers bred for hunting have shorter coats than cockers bred for dog shows. The coat comes in many colors.

Behavior

Cocker spaniels help bird hunters. The dogs find birds and chase them from their hiding spots. Cockers are smart. They have lots of energy. They are gentle and happy dogs. Cockers love kids and other dogs.

Height: 13.5 to 15.5 inches (34.2 to 39.4 cm) at the shoulders

Weight: 20 to 30 pounds (9 to 14 kg)

Pacific Ocean

Canada

United States

Atlantic Ocean

Mexico

From: The United States of America

English springers bred for shows have more fur than those bred for working.

English Springer Spaniel

AKC Date: 1910

Appearance

English springer spaniels have long, floppy ears. They have short docked tails. These dogs have

medium-length double coats. The coat comes in mixes of black, liver, white, and tan.

Height: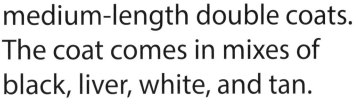
19 to 20 inches (48 to 51 cm) at the shoulders

Weight:
40 to 50 pounds (18 to 23 kg)

Behavior

English springer spaniels chase birds from hiding and retrieve them for hunters. They have lots of energy. These dogs want to please people. They are easy to train. They are friendly and love their families. They like to swim.

Scotland

Northern Ireland

Ireland

England

Wales

Atlantic Ocean

From: England

This breed will get bored with long training sessions.

German Shorthaired Pointer

AKC Date: 1930

Appearance

German shorthaired pointers (GSPs) have floppy ears. They have short, smooth fur. The coat comes in solid liver or solid black. It can also be

in patterns of liver and white or black and white. The tail is docked.

Height:
21 to 25 inches (53 to 64 cm) at the shoulders

Weight:
45 to 70 pounds (20 to 32 kg)

Behavior

GSPs point and retrieve birds. They also hunt animals like rabbits and deer. These dogs are smart and full of energy. They are friendly. GSPs like kids. They make good watchdogs. They love to swim.

North Sea
Denmark
Baltic Sea
The Netherlands
Poland
Belgium
Germany
Czechia
Luxembourg
France Switzerland
Austria

From: Germany

Goldens are good with other dogs.

Golden Retriever

AKC Date: 1925

Appearance

Golden retrievers have medium-length double coats. They come in shades of gold. The fur is water resistant. These dogs have short ears that hang down. Their tails are long.

Height: 21.5 to 24 inches (54.6 to 61 cm) at the shoulders

Weight: 55 to 75 pounds (25 to 34 kg)

Behavior

Goldens retrieve birds such as geese and ducks for hunters. Goldens are easy to train. They are friendly and love their families and kids. These dogs are good swimmers. Goldens often work in search and rescue. They are also common service dogs and guide dogs for people who are blind.

Scotland

Northern Ireland

Ireland

England

Wales

Atlantic Ocean

From: Scotland

The Irish setter needs regular combing.

Irish Setter

AKC Date: 1878

Appearance

Irish setters have medium-length fur. It can be red, mahogany, or chestnut. Their floppy ears are long. This breed's legs are long and strong. The tail has long fur.

Height:
25 to 27 inches
(64 to 69 cm) at the
shoulders

Weight:
60 to 70 pounds
(27 to 32 kg)

Behavior

Irish setters help hunt birds. They set, or crouch, to show where birds are. These fun-loving dogs have lots of energy. They are sweet and friendly. They are very good with kids and other dogs. The Irish setter wants to please but also wants to have its own way.

Northern
Ireland

Ireland

Great
Britain

Atlantic Ocean

From: Ireland and
Northern Ireland

In 2021, the Labrador retriever was the most popular breed in the United States for the thirtieth year in a row.

Labrador Retriever

AKC Date: 1917

Appearance

The Labrador retriever has a short double coat. It can be black, yellow, or chocolate. The Lab's coat keeps it warm in cold water. Its tail is called an otter tail because it is thick. Labs' webbed toes help them swim.

Height:
21.5 to
24.5 inches
(54.6 to 62.2 cm) at
the shoulders

Weight:
55 to 80 pounds
(25 to 36 kg)

Behavior

Labs retrieve birds such as ducks for hunters. Labs want to please their owners. They are good with kids and other dogs. They love to swim. Labs often work as service dogs. They also work with police and the military. They like food and can gain weight easily.

From: Canada

Lagotto Romagnolo

AKC Date: 2015

Appearance

The Lagotto Romagnolo (lah-GO-toh row-man-YO-low) has a long, curly coat. The coat comes in off-white, white, and shades of brown and orange.

Behavior

The Lagotto is often used to find truffles, a type of edible fungus. These dogs have lots of energy.

Height: 🔲
16 to 19 inches
(41 to 48 cm) at the shoulders

Weight: 🏋
24 to 35 pounds
(11 to 16 kg)

Switzerland Austria Slovenia
France Italy Croatia Bosnia & Herzegovina
Mediterranean Sea

From: Italy

Vizsla

AKC Date: 1960

Appearance

The vizsla (VEESH-luh) has a short, golden-rust coat. Its nose and eyes are the same color as the coat. The ears are large and floppy. The breed's tail is docked long.

Height: 21 to 24 inches (53 to 61 cm) at the shoulders

Weight: 44 to 60 pounds (20 to 27 kg)

Behavior

Vizlas hunt birds and waterfowl. They can point and retrieve. These dogs are fast. They have lots of energy and need exercise. They love their families.

From: Hungary

Another name for this breed is the Korthals griffon.

Wirehaired Pointing Griffon

AKC Date: 1887

Appearance

The wirehaired pointing griffon (grih-FAWN) has a medium-length wiry coat. It comes in brown and gray or chestnut and gray. The coat can have white hairs mixed in. The tail is docked.

Height:
20 to 24 inches
(51 to 61 cm) at the
shoulders

Weight:
35 to 70 pounds
(16 to 32 kg)

Behavior
These dogs can help with
all types of hunting. They
can follow an animal's
scent, point, and retrieve.
They have lots of energy.
They are smart and
easy to train. They love
their families. They are
great swimmers.

The
Netherlands

United
Kingdom

Germany

Belgium

France

Switzerland

Atlantic
Ocean

Italy

Spain

From: France and
the Netherlands

American Water Spaniel

From: The United States

Behavior: American water spaniels need to keep busy. They are friendly.

Chesapeake Bay Retriever

From: The United States

Behavior: These dogs are loyal. They can be protective.

English Setter

From: England

Behavior: English setters help hunters. They find birds and point. They are gentle.

Nova Scotia Duck Tolling Retriever

From: Canada

Behavior: These dogs bounce close to shore. This attracts ducks for hunters. Tollers are smart. They need lots of exercise.

Pointer

From: England

Behavior: Pointers are full of energy. They need lots of exercise.

Weimaraner

From: Germany

Behavior: The Weimaraner (WY-muh-rah-nur) needs lots of exercise. It can be protective.

The Airedale terrier is called the "king of the terriers."

Airedale Terrier

AKC Date: 1888

Appearance

Airedale (AIR-dale) terriers are the largest dogs in the Terrier Group.

Scotland

Northern Ireland

Ireland

England

Wales

Atlantic Ocean

From: England

They have long heads. Their ears are folded. This breed's coat is wiry. It comes in black and tan or grizzle and tan. This dog has a beard and long legs.

Height: 23 inches (58 cm) at the shoulders

Weight: 50 to 70 pounds (23 to 32 kg)

Behavior

Airedale terriers hunt birds, waterfowl, and furred prey. They work hard and have lots of energy. They are brave. These dogs can be protective, but they are usually friendly. They are smart and sometimes stubborn.

Bedlington Terrier

AKC Date: 1886

Appearance

Bedlington terriers look like lambs. They have curly fur. The fur does not shed. These dogs have long heads and arched backs.

Height: 15 to 17.5 inches (38 to 44.5 cm) at the shoulders

Weight: 17 to 23 pounds (8 to 10 kg)

Behavior

Bedlington terriers hunt animals such as rats. They have lots of energy. They are brave. These dogs make good watchdogs.

Scotland

Northern Ireland

Ireland

England

Wales

Atlantic Ocean

From: England

Border Terrier

AKC Date: 1930

Appearance

The Border terrier has a head that looks like an otter. The dog has wiry fur. The coat comes in red, wheaten, blue and tan, and grizzle and tan.

Height: 12 to 15 inches (31 to 38 cm) at the shoulders

Weight: 11.5 to 15.5 pounds (5.2 to 7 kg)

Behavior

Border terriers were first bred to hunt foxes. They are happy and friendly. They will chase small animals. Border terriers have lots of energy. They like to dig.

From: England and Scotland

Bull Terrier

AKC Date: 1885

Appearance

Bull terriers are muscular. This breed has an egg-shaped head. Its eyes are shaped like triangles. The coat is short and smooth. It comes in many colors.

Height: 21 to 22 inches (53 to 56 cm) at the shoulders

Weight: 50 to 70 pounds (23 to 32 kg)

Behavior

Bull terriers have lots of energy. They need exercise. They are playful and silly. These dogs are loyal to their owners.

Scotland

Northern Ireland

Ireland

England

Wales

Atlantic Ocean

From: England

Cairn Terrier

AKC Date: 1913

Appearance

The cairn terrier has a short, wide head. It has pricked ears. This dog has short legs. Its medium-length wiry coat comes in many colors.

Behavior

Cairn terriers were first bred to hunt rodents and foxes. They are smart. They want to keep busy. They need exercise. These dogs are happy. They like to dig.

Height: 9.5 to 10 inches (24.1 to 25 cm) at the shoulders

Weight: 13 to 14 pounds (5.9 to 6.4 kg)

Scotland
Northern Ireland
Ireland
England
Wales
Atlantic Ocean

From: Scotland

Miniature schnauzers can make good pets in the city.

Miniature Schnauzer

AKC Date: 1926

Appearance

The miniature schnauzer is the smallest of the schnauzers. It has hairy eyebrows, a mustache, and a beard. The tail is docked. The dog has a medium-length wiry coat. It does not shed.

The coat comes in colors of salt and pepper, black and silver, and solid black.

Behavior

Miniature schnauzers were first bred to hunt rats. These dogs are smart and brave. They bark a lot, making them good watchdogs. Miniature schnauzers will chase small animals. They are friendly, energetic, and playful.

Height: 12 to 14 inches (31 to 36 cm) at the shoulders

Weight: 11 to 20 pounds (5 to 9 kg)

From: Germany

This breed's fur needs lots of combing.

Soft-Coated Wheaten Terrier

AKC Date: 1973

Appearance

The soft-coated wheaten terrier has

Northern Ireland

Ireland

Great Britain

Atlantic Ocean

From: Ireland and Northern Ireland

a long head. Its coat is long, silky, and wavy. It comes in shades of wheat. It does not shed much. The coat falls over the dog's eyes. The tail is docked.

Behavior

Wheatens were first bred to do many jobs on the farm. They hunted rats and guarded farm animals. They make great watchdogs. These dogs are friendly and loyal. They are happy. They love their families.

Height:
17 to 19 inches
(43 to 48 cm) at the shoulders

Weight:
30 to 40 pounds
(14 to 18 kg)

Staffies enjoy training.

Staffordshire Bull Terrier

AKC Date: 1974

Appearance

The Staffordshire bull terrier (Staffie) is muscular. It has a short head. It has big

Scotland

Northern Ireland

England

Ireland

Wales

Atlantic Ocean

From: England

cheek muscles. The coat is smooth and short. It comes in many colors. It can be brindle.

Behavior

Staffordshire bull terriers are tough and brave. They make good watchdogs. Staffies usually do not get along well with dogs or other animals. They are often called nanny dogs because they love kids. These dogs are smart and active. They like doing things with their families.

Height:
14 to 16 inches
(36 to 41 cm) at the shoulders

Weight:
24 to 38 pounds
(11 to 17 kg)

West Highland White Terrier

AKC Date: 1908

Appearance

The West Highland white terrier (Westie) has a medium-length wiry coat. The coat is solid white. This breed's eyes are dark, and its nose is black. The dog has thick eyebrows. An adult's small ears

stand up straight. The tail is shaped like a carrot.

Behavior

Westies were first bred to hunt rodents. They are smart and get bored easily. They are friendly and can be goofy. They love their families. They will chase small animals.

Height:
10 to 11 inches
(25 to 28 cm) at the shoulders

Weight:
15 to 20 pounds
(7 to 9 kg)

Scotland

Northern Ireland

Ireland

England

Wales

Atlantic Ocean

From: Scotland

Australian Terrier

From: Australia

Behavior: Australian terriers are brave dogs. They like to dig.

Kerry Blue Terrier

From: Ireland

Behavior: These gray-coated dogs are smart. They are playful and will chase small animals.

Manchester Terrier (Standard)

From: England

Behavior: Manchester terriers are brave and loyal. They make good watchdogs.

Scottish Terrier

From: Scotland

Behavior: Scottish terriers are strong-willed. They chase other animals.

Skye Terrier

From: Scotland

Behavior: These long, short dogs are brave and tough. They take a while to become friends with new people. These dogs are calm compared to other terriers.

Smooth Fox Terrier

From: England

Behavior: Smooth fox terriers are fast. They are friendly. They like to bark. They make good watchdogs.

Cavalier King Charles Spaniel

AKC Date: 1995

Appearance

The Cavalier King Charles spaniel has a silky and wavy coat.

The Cavalier should not be trimmed for shows, but dogs not showing can be trimmed.

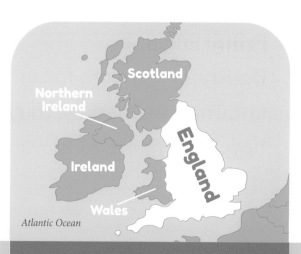

Scotland

Northern Ireland

Ireland

England

Wales

Atlantic Ocean

From: England

It comes in white with chestnut markings, black and white with tan markings, ruby, and black and tan. These dogs have floppy ears that hang down. Their eyes are large and round. The tail has long fur.

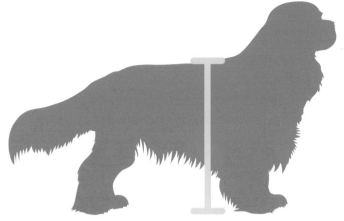

Height:
12 to 13 inches
(31 to 33 cm) at the shoulders

Weight:
13 to 18 pounds
(6 to 8 kg)

Behavior

Cavalier King Charles spaniels are gentle. They are friendly to strangers. They love their families. Cavaliers also love kids. They are happy to be calm or active with their owners. These dogs are easy to train.

This breed is named for the Mexican state of Chihuahua.

Chihuahua

AKC Date: 1904

Appearance

The Chihuahua (chee-WAH-wah) has a head shaped like an apple. Its muzzle is pointed.

United States of America

Mexico

Gulf of Mexico

Pacific Ocean

Guatemala

Belize

From: Mexico

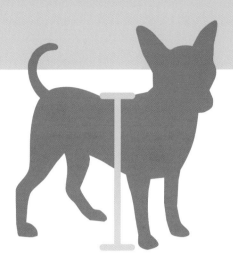

Its ears are pricked. This dog has large, round eyes. The tail is curved. These dogs can have short or long coats. The coat comes in many colors.

Height: 5 to 8 inches (13 to 20 cm) at the shoulders

Weight: Under 6 pounds (2.7 kg)

Behavior

Chihuahuas are brave and loyal. They make good watchdogs. They will stand up to any animal. It does not matter how big the animal is. Chihuahuas are sassy. They like to travel. They are good at training their owners.

Chinese Crested

AKC Date: 1991

Appearance

Chinese cresteds can be mostly hairless, with silky hair on the head, tail, and lower legs. Others have silky hair all over. The coats come in many colors.

Behavior

Chinese cresteds are happy and playful. They are loyal. These dogs love their families. They are easy to train.

Height:
11 to 13 inches
(28 to 33 cm) at the shoulders

Weight:
8 to 12 pounds
(3.6 to 5 kg)

From: China

Papillon

AKC Date: 1915

Appearance

The papillon (pah-pee-YOHN) can have pricked ears that look like the wings of a butterfly. Other papillons have floppy ears. The coat is medium length and silky. The coat comes in a mix of white and other colors.

Height: 🗍
8 to 11 inches (20 to 28 cm) at the shoulders

Weight: ⚖
5 to 10 pounds (2.3 to 5 kg)

Behavior

Papillons are smart and agile. They do well in dog sports. They are happy and friendly.

From: Belgium and France

Pomeranians can learn tricks quickly.

Pomeranian

AKC Date: 1888

Appearance

The Pomeranian has a face that looks like a fox. It has small, pricked ears. It has a

Baltic Sea
Lithuania
Germany
Poland
Czechia
Slovakia
France
Austria

From: Germany and Poland

short muzzle. These dogs have long double coats. The coats come in many colors, such as blue merle, orange, or black and tan. The fur is fluffy around the neck. The tail is fluffy too.

Height: 6 to 7 inches (15 to 18 cm) at the shoulders

Weight: 3 to 7 pounds (1.4 to 3.2 kg)

Behavior

Pomeranians are related to sled dogs. They are bold and brave. They make good watchdogs. Poms love their families. They like to cuddle. They enjoy going places with their owners.

A pug's wrinkles need to be frequently wiped.

Pug

AKC Date: 1885

Appearance

Pugs have big, round heads. They have flat faces with wrinkles. Their eyes are big. Some people think

Kazakhstan　Russia

Mongolia

North Korea

China

South Korea

India

Burma

Vietnam

Pacific Ocean

From: China

these dogs have human-like faces. This dog has a short, smooth coat. The coat comes in fawn with a black mask. It can also be solid black. The tail curls over the back.

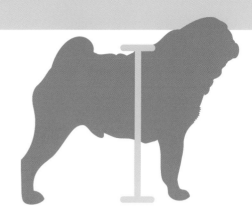

Height:
10 to 13 inches
(25 to 33 cm) at the shoulders

Weight:
14 to 18 pounds
(6 to 8 kg)

Behavior

Pugs are playful and friendly. They love their families. They are gentle and quiet. They are not good swimmers. They like food and can gain weight easily.

A short haircut on a shih tzu is easier to care for than a long show coat.

Shih Tzu

AKC Date: 1969

Appearance

The shih tzu (SHEET ZOO) has long fur. The coat is silky. It comes in many colors

From: China

and patterns. These dogs have large, round eyes. The shih tzu has a short muzzle. It has a fluffy tail.

Behavior

Shih tzus are friendly. They are playful. They are good with kids and other dogs. But children must be gentle with puppies. The puppies' small size means they can get hurt easily. Shih tzus enjoy cuddles. These dogs make good therapy dogs. They travel well.

Height:
9 to 10.5 inches (23 to 26.7 cm) at the shoulders

Weight:
9 to 16 pounds (4.1 to 7 kg)

Yorkshire Terrier

AKC Date: 1885

The Yorkie's long hair needs to be kept out of its eyes.

Appearance

The Yorkshire terrier (Yorkie) has a long, silky coat. It can grow to the floor. The coat

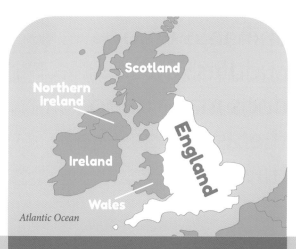

Scotland

Northern Ireland

Ireland

England

Wales

Atlantic Ocean

From: England

comes in blue and tan, blue and gold, black and tan, or black and gold. It does not shed much. The tail is docked to a medium length. The ears are pricked.

Height: 7 to 8 inches (18 to 20 cm) at the shoulders

Weight: 7 pounds (3.2 kg)

Behavior

Yorkies were first used to hunt rats. They are brave. They like to bark. They make good watchdogs. They love their families and enjoy cuddling. They need to be handled gently because of their small size. Yorkies do well in dog sports.

Affenpinscher

From: Germany

Behavior: Affenpinschers were first used as ratters. They are brave. Sometimes they are silly.

Italian Greyhound

From: Greece and Turkey, possibly

Behavior: Italian greyhounds are tiny sight hounds. They will chase small animals. They are playful. They enjoy being cuddled.

Maltese

From: Malta

Behavior: Maltese are gentle and loving. They like to cuddle. They are playful.

Miniature Pinscher

From: Germany

Behavior: Miniature pinschers are brave. They make good watchdogs. They are loyal to their families.

Pekingese

From: China

Behavior: Pekingese are loyal to their families. They make good watchdogs. These flat-faced dogs are loving.

Toy Fox Terrier

From: The United States of America

Behavior: Fox terriers were first used as ratters. They are brave and playful. These dogs are also smart and friendly.

These dogs shed a lot.

Bernese Mountain Dog

AKC Date: 1937

Appearance

The Bernese mountain dog has a thick double coat. The coat is medium length. It comes in black, tan, and white. The coat sheds a lot. This dog's body is powerful.

Behavior

Bernese mountain dogs were first bred to work on farms. They moved cattle and pulled carts. They are strong but gentle. They like kids and other dogs. They love cold weather. Like with other large dogs, early training is important. These dogs must learn how to behave around people.

Height: 23 to 27.5 inches (58 to 69.9 cm) at the shoulders

Weight: 70 to 115 pounds (32 to 52 kg)

Germany

Austria

Switzerland

France

Italy

From: Switzerland

The breed may have gotten its name because it often uses its front paws to box while playing.

Boxer

AKC Date: 1904

Appearance

The boxer is muscular. It has a square jaw and a short, wide muzzle. It has an underbite. These dogs' ears can be cropped and sit straight up. Natural ears are floppy. The coat is short.

Height: 📏
21.5 to 25 inches
(54.6 to 64 cm) at
the shoulders

Weight: ⚖️
50 to 80 pounds
(23 to 36 kg)

It comes in shades of fawn or brindle. The dogs can have white markings and a black mask. The boxer has a docked tail.

Behavior

Boxers are smart. They are playful and energetic, so they are called the "Peter Pan" of dogs. They love and protect their families, especially children.

From: Germany

The plural form of the breed's name is cani corsi.

Cane Corso

AKC Date: 2010

Appearance

The cane corso (KAH-nay KOR-so) is muscular. It has a big head. The short coat

Switzerland
Austria
Slovenia
France
Italy
Croatia
Bosnia & Herzegovina
Mediterranean Sea

From: Italy

comes in black and shades of gray, fawn, and red. This dog can have a black or gray mask.

Behavior

The cane corso is smart. These dogs are brave and loyal. They are protective. They make great guard dogs. They need to have a job to do. They need a lot of training from a young age. This will help them be gentle around people. They are easy to train.

Height:
23.5 to 27.5 inches (59.7 to 69.9 cm) at the shoulders

Weight:
Usually over 100 pounds (45 kg)

The giant schnauzer is the biggest schnauzer breed.

Giant Schnauzer

AKC Date: 1930

Appearance

The giant schnauzer has a head shaped like a rectangle.

North Sea

Denmark

Baltic Sea

The Netherlands

Belgium

Luxembourg

France

Germany

Poland

Czechia

Austria

Switzerland

From: Germany

It has bushy eyebrows and a beard. This dog has a medium-length wiry coat. The coat comes in solid black or salt and pepper. The tail is docked.

Height: 23 to 27.5 inches (58 to 69.9 cm) at the shoulders

Weight: 55 to 85 pounds (25 to 39 kg)

Behavior

Giant schnauzers were first used to move cattle and protect farm animals. They are brave and loyal. They make good guard dogs. They are smart. They need a job to do. These dogs do well in dog sports, such as pulling carts and herding.

Great Dane

AKC Date: 1887

Appearance

The Great Dane is tall. This dog has a short, smooth coat. The coat comes in many colors. One of the coat colors is called harlequin. It is white with black patches. The ears can be cropped or left floppy.

Height: 28 to 32 inches (71 to 81 cm) at the shoulders

Weight: 110 to 175 pounds (50 to 79 kg)

Behavior

Great Danes are brave and loyal. They make good watchdogs. These dogs are gentle and friendly.

From: Germany

Great Pyrenees

AKC Date: 1933

Appearance

The Great Pyrenees has a thick double coat. The coat is white. It can have gray, tan, badger, or reddish-brown markings.

Behavior

Great Pyrenees guard sheep from predators such as wolves. They are brave and strong. They can bark a lot. Great Pyrenees love their families.

Height:
25 to 32 inches
(64 to 81 cm) at the shoulders

Weight:
85 pounds
(39 kg) and up

From: France

Mastiffs drool a lot.

Mastiff

AKC Date: 1885

Appearance

The mastiff is muscular. It has a huge head. It has wrinkles on the forehead. The lips hang down. The ears are small and floppy. The mastiff has a short double coat. The coat comes in apricot, brindle, and fawn. The face has a black mask.

Behavior

Mastiffs were first used to hunt large animals. They also guarded homes. These dogs are strong and brave. They make good watchdogs. They are gentle and calm. They do not need much exercise for their size. But daily walks will help them stay healthy.

Height: 27.5 inches (69.9 cm) and up

Weight: 120 to 230 pounds (54 to 104 kg)

From: England

Newfoundland

AKC Date: 1886

Appearance

The Newfoundland's webbed feet help it swim. The double coat is thick and helps the dog stay dry. The coat comes in black, brown, and gray, with or without white.

Height:
26 to 28 inches
(66 to 71 cm) at the shoulders

Weight:
100 to 150 pounds
(45 to 68 kg)

Behavior

Newfoundlands work in water. They love to swim. Newfoundlands are strong and brave. They are sweet and gentle. They are great with kids.

Canada

Pacific Ocean

United States of America

Atlantic Ocean

From: Canada

Portuguese Water Dog

AKC Date: 1983

Appearance

The Portuguese water dog has a long coat that can be curly or wavy. It comes in black, white, or brown. The coat can have white markings.

Behavior

Portuguese water dogs love the water. These dogs have lots of energy. They are smart and need a job to do.

Height:
17 to 23 inches (43 to 58 cm) at the shoulders

Weight:
35 to 60 pounds (16 to 27 kg)

Portugal

Spain

Atlantic Ocean

Morocco

From: Portugal

Siberian huskies enjoy chewing and digging.

Siberian Husky

AKC Date: 1930

Appearance

The Siberian husky has a face that looks like a fox. It has pricked ears. The dog's

Arctic Ocean
Finland
Russia
Ukraine
China
Mongolia
Kazakhstan

From: Russia

eyes can be blue, brown, or one of each color. These dogs have thick double coats. The coats come in many different colors. The tail is bushy.

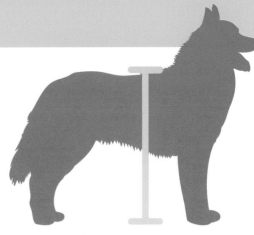

Height: 20 to 23.5 inches (51 to 59.7 cm) at the shoulders

Weight: 35 to 60 pounds (16 to 27 kg)

Behavior

Siberian huskies pull sleds across ice and snow. They are fast and need to run. They will chase small animals. Huskies are friendly. They love their families. They like other dogs. This breed often howls and makes other sounds.

Akita

From: Japan
Behavior: Akitas are very loyal and protective. They are brave.

Doberman Pinscher

From: Germany
Behavior: Doberman pinschers are smart and loyal. They are good watchdogs. They often work as police or military dogs.

Leonberger

From: Germany
Behavior: These huge dogs are gentle and calm. They are friendly. They love their families.

Rottweiler

From: Germany

Behavior: Rottweilers are loyal and brave. They make good guard dogs. They work with police and the military.

Saint Bernard

From: Switzerland

Behavior: Saint Bernards are huge and strong. They are gentle and calm. They love children so much that they are often called nanny dogs. They drool a lot.

Samoyed

From: Russia

Behavior: The Samoyed (sam-ah-YED) is smart. It is loyal and gentle. These dogs like to stay busy.

GLOSSARY

agile
Able to turn quickly and easily.

bred
Brought two animals together to have young.

breed
A group of animals that looks and acts similarly.

brindle
A striped pattern on a dog's coat.

cropped
Had the ears cut by a veterinarian so they stand upright.

docked
Had a portion of the tail removed by a veterinarian.

double coat
A coat with a top layer of longer fur that covers an under layer of shorter, softer fur.

independent
Good at being alone and making decisions alone.

mask
Coloring on a dog's face that is darker than on most of the body.

merle
A pattern of reddish or blueish gray mixed with spots of darker colors.

point
To stand still with the muzzle pointing toward prey.

prey
An animal that is hunted by other animals.

pricked
Ears that stand upright.

scent hound
A dog that finds and follows prey mainly by using its sense of smell.

sight hound
A dog that finds and follows prey mainly by using its sense of sight.

underbite
A lower jaw that extends in front of the upper jaw.

TO LEARN MORE

More Books to Read

Hughes, Catherine D. *Little Kids First Big Book of Pets*. National Geographic Kids, 2019.

Mills, Andrea. *The Everything Book of Dogs and Puppies*. DK, 2018.

Murray, Julie. *Dogs*. Abdo, 2019.

Online Resources

Booklinks
NONFICTION NETWORK
FREE! ONLINE NONFICTION RESOURCES

To learn more about dogs, please visit **abdobooklinks.com** or scan this QR code. These links are routinely monitored and updated to provide the most current information available.

INDEX

PHOTO CREDITS